What are they talking about?

This book is dedicated to
the Reverend G. W. Thompson
and his wife Dorothy
who provided the firm foundation for my life

My grateful thanks are due to
the Reverend Neville Barker Cryer, M.A.
who gave much kindly help and advice
in the preparation of this book

and also to
Steve Lingham
who kindly drew
the illustrations

Printed in 12 on 13 point Times typeface
by Sessions of York
The Ebor Press
York

Published by Thompson-Morelane Publishing
4 Moor Lane, Haxby
York YO32 2PH

This book explains some of the words used in Christian worship. It could be helpful for Christians, and for anyone who would like to get to know what they are talking about.

Regular Christian worshippers say the words so often that they may forget what they really mean.

Anyone who does not often go to church services might find their language very confusing.

So there is a real need for a small book like this.

Whilst it is possible to over-simplify, the ideas need to be explained in a way which is easy to understand at this stage.

This book, therefore, is not intended to explain the whole of the Christian faith, just to put a bit of meaning into some of the words which are used.

In this book, we shall follow the general pattern of the Communion services suggested for the Church of England, of which there are several variations. This does not mean, however, being limited to any one version of Christianity.

The words appear in any form of Christian worship, and it is important that we understand them.

There is an A-W list at the back for anyone who prefers to look up words individually.

The first two words are probably the most difficult, so if you find them too heavy for you, keep going, the rest of the book is easy to understand and may provide you with some amusement too!

1

Many of our services start with
*'The **Lord** be with you', or 'The **Lord** is here'.*
*(Or we say the '**Lord's** Prayer'.)*
Lord.
Ordinary Jewish people were not allowed to pronounce the proper name of God. The reason for this was that the **name** was the same as the true identity.
*(See also under the section '**Name**').*
As nobody could dare to claim to know the whole identity of God, the name was not to be used.
Certain other words were used instead.
Lord was one of the words which was substituted.
So these days, when we say "The Lord be with you", what we are really saying is "God be with you."
With a small 'L', the word has always been used for kings and for anyone who rules over others, especially as it was thought that kings ruled for God on the earth.
So when we use the word, it is also helps us to bear in mind the **authority** of the God about whom we are talking.
What, then, is this God?
Is God some sort of invention of the human mind? Is this a God whose character we decide for ourselves?
For some people, God does seem to be something like that. They think of God as being a grandfatherly magician, who loves us and can see us safely across the road, even if we step out in the path of a large bus!
Ancient civilisations, even the most primitive, have had an idea of the existence of thinking forces beyond the human mind. These 'Gods' were either friendly or hostile. Some of them could be persuaded to be nice if people were good or kind, especially if they gave gifts to the Gods.
Sadly, a lot of these ideas have stuck with us, and still affect our thinking today.

The early Jews, as represented in Abraham, had the idea that, instead of there being a whole army of 'Gods', each for a different aspect of human life, (such as God of War, God of Love, God of Drink etc.) there was really only one God. This God was thought of as being the creative force
 - the very start of everything which exists.
The Bible begins with a story of the creation of the world and the part which humans are meant to have in it.
If we accept that God is a thinking creative power, indeed THE thinking creative power, it helps us to look at things in a completely new way. This God made our world to run on certain principles, such as that of reproduction, or survival, and a way in which things evolve gradually.
To survive, things must be renewed, change and develop.
So if we are going to survive, we need to be ready to change and develop along the lines which God has laid down.
There will be various spin-offs from this idea as we consider evil, sin etc., but for now let us at least be sure that we are not making up a God of our own; that we are ready to accept and worship the one true God, even if we don't always like some of God's ideas! Few of us like pain, but we should be in a bad way if we could not feel any pain.
We don't like wasps because they sting us.
But our dislikes are often the result of our ignorance.
So it is right to start our worship by concentrating our minds on the fact that the one true God is right here with us.

We say a prayer of preparation, beginning with....
Almighty *God.....*
Almighty.

It is very hard to imagine a God who is **all mighty**, that is to say, who has power over everything. People ask "If God is almighty, why does God let bad things happen?"

It depends on how you understand God.

If God is the creative force behind all that has been made, we have to accept the way in which things have been made, not make them into what **we** would want.

So cancer exists. It is one of the ways in which nature gets rid of things, as is heart failure, and the various different diseases. To say they ought not to exist is to tell God that things were made wrongly. God made a developing world, one in which cancer and other diseases may well cease to exist one day. But even if those don't exist, other things will still be there to remove people from the earth.

If God is almighty, why not speed it up, to save us pain?

For the same reason. The world was created to develop slowly, to progress towards perfection. If God made it perfect now, it would not be the same place at all. It would be static and totally boring. What would our characters be like then? So we should not try to make God into a different God when we don't like some of the things which are done.

You can't wave a magic wand to alter a world not designed to run on magic.

If you constructed a little toy which learnt from experience that banging into things was painful, with the result that the pain stopped it from repeating the mistake, are you then a bad creator? If you felt that it was unkind to let the toy feel pain, you would be forced to get rid of the original toy and redesign it. Then it would not be the same toy. God does not think of us as 'toys' but even being all-powerful does not let you escape the total logic of that situation.

So there is a moment at which a creator is bound by the logic of the creation. The creator is only all-powerful in that there is the choice to leave it or to destroy it and start again.

Although we humans are for ever 'up-grading' our imperfect inventions, God has already built in the ways of 'up-grading' and cannot for ever be tinkering and upsetting that pattern. When we use our knowledge in keeping with God's plan, we help to do some of the 'up-grading'. Fortunately, if we spoil the plans, the system is usually able to reassert itself once the irritation has been got rid of. God is still a personal God and is always ready to help us to see what we should be doing, and how we should be doing it.

The reason why so many of us find it hard to understand is that, as we said, people try to make their own idea of God, and what God should be like.

In most of the Bible, the translation 'almighty' is used for the word 'shaddai'

which really just means 'mighty' or 'powerful'.

But the writer of Revelation uses the Greek word meaning '**all**-powerful' because it fits in better with the symbolic picture he is trying to give.

Please God, make three eights twenty-seven, otherwise my maths test will be all wrong!

Now read on!

How almighty can you get?

.....cleanse the **thoughts of our hearts.....**
Thoughts of our hearts.
Our hearts may not have 'thoughts' if we see things from the medical standpoint, but it is quite clear that the word 'heart' is often used in modern English to represent our personality and our emotions. (We say someone is 'good-hearted'.)
In the Bible, the 'heart' could represent all that makes us a real person - the way we **think**, and even our conscience.

.....by the inspiration of Your Holy **Spirit.....**
Spirit.
This word is also one surrounded by much superstition and ignorance, from early times up to today.
One of its first meanings was the idea of 'breath' or 'movement of air'. It is one way of describing the life force which keeps us going. This is more than the beating of the heart, and all that keeps us physically alive. It is the living force which makes us creative and alive as people.
If that is too hard to understand, think of it as our basic attitude to life, influencing all that we do and all that we are.
So the spirit of **God**, is the creative force itself, which keeps everything alive, not just physically but as positive, creative forces, working with God. We shall discuss elsewhere the idea of 'evil', but of course **'evil spirits'** are forces which drive us to act contrary to the pattern of God. If we allow the wrong spirit to colour our view of life, we are cut off from all that is creatively good, because all goodness then has no more effect on us than does water on a duck's back. This is why Jesus made such a point of saying that we can do, or say, wrong things and still be forgiven, but if we get the wrong spirit we are going to be totally lost, unless we are somehow able to regain the true spirit of God. We may, for example, regain it by God's grace. (*See under* **'Grace'**).

So it is also very important that we begin our worship by reminding ourselves, not only that God is present, but of the importance of being in the right spirit, without which all our worship will be spoiled.

.....by the **inspiration** *of Your Holy Spirit*

Inspiration.

This word contains the idea of being 'breathed into'.

After what we have just said about the 'spirit' being a word associated with the idea of breath, it is natural that we should be 'inspired' by the Holy Spirit.

The word 'inspire' is often used in the world today to mean that we get a sudden bright idea which we have not worked out for ourselves. It is like having a new idea 'breathed' into our mind.

Whilst the Spirit docs give us some good ideas, that is not really what 'inspiration' means in this Communion service. Here we are asking God to fill us with (or to breathe into us) that Spirit which is a positive, creative force and which keeps us in tune with God.

Not everybody seemed to approach the services at St. Giles' in quite the same spirit!

.....by the inspiration of Your **Holy** *Spirit*

Holy.

People sometimes seem to think that the word 'holy' means being all smug and 'goody-goody'.

But this is very far from its real meaning as used in the Bible and in our services. The original idea behind the word is that of being ....

 ....**separate**

- not part of the general run of things.

God is very special, and not confined to our everyday world, so is thought of as being 'holy'.

As a result, things which are touched by God are also given God's 'specialness', and may therefore be called 'holy'.

Just as the word 'Lord' is given a big letter when it applies to God, (and 'God' is given a big letter too) the word 'Holy' may also be given a big letter when it relates to God.

In the Jewish faith, the 'Holy of Holies' was the most special place of all, the place of God's presence. It was so special that nobody could go in there except the High Priest. In our modern churches, we have more or less given up the idea of any place being especially 'Holy', as we think of God as being everywhere.

On the other hand, there is nothing wrong with keeping a place 'special' for meeting God, which is why we have church buildings. We may even keep a particular area inside a church as 'special' if we want to do so.

We have just discussed the word 'Spirit', and so the **Holy** Spirit, is that Spirit which is special to God.

We ask that we may be given the **Holy** Spirit, rather than other spirits which are not special to God.

.....**perfectly** *love you.....*
Perfect.
This means 'complete and without shortcomings or flaws'.
We pray that our love may be complete and unspoilt.

.....*perfectly* **love** *you.....*
Love.
This word can mean almost anything in popular jargon.
Some people 'love' fish and chips. People who are 'in love'
may be showing sentimental feelings, or physical attraction.
Parents who 'love' their children may think it means heaping
very expensive things on them. (Even though it may in fact
prove to be just the opposite of love in the end!).
People who say that they 'love' animals may mean that they
lavish affection on them. But that sort of 'love' may be more
for the owner's pleasure than for that of the animals.
Christian love consists of **wanting the best** for the person
who is loved. It may involve the other sorts of 'love', or not.
A parent who loves a child will not be so lavish with lots of
'lovely' things to eat that the child's health is ruined.
Those who love their dog will not sit and cuddle it all day,
but will take it for exercise on long walks in all weathers.
So, oddly enough, to 'love' people may even mean 'telling
them off' sometimes, or getting them to do something which
is really good for them, even if they do not like it!
Sometimes, love may involve sharing grief and showing
sympathy. At other times, it may mean helping someone to
regain his or her sense of humour, or to get on with living in
a positive way, without too much bitterness or self-pity.
When we 'love' God, we want what is best for God's plans,
that God's Will may be done on earth, and when we say that
God 'loves' us, we mean that God wants the best for us.
That is why Jesus came to show us what **is** best for us.

.....and worthily **magnify** *Your* .....

Magnify.

Today, this word means to make something bigger. So you have a 'magnifying' glass to make print etc. look bigger.

But the word comes from a Latin word 'magnus' which means 'great', or 'large'. So here the word 'magnify' means 'to see the **greatness** of'.

In this prayer, we are saying that we want to recognise the greatness of God for all that it is truly worth, ('**worthily**').

.....Your Holy **Name.**

Name.

To many civilisations, the **name** which a person was given was more than just a way of identifying him or her.

The name was thought of as being an expression of the true character of that person.

So God could not be talked about by 'name', because nobody can really understand the true nature of God. This is why the Israelites were forbidden to use the real 'name' of God, (*as we saw under the word* **'Lord'**).

It explains why people in the Old Testament were so keen to know the 'name' of God - they wanted to know the true character of God. In this prayer, we say that we fully value the greatness of God's special character, or 'Holy Name'.

.....through **Christ**, *our Lord.*

Christ.

People have got into the habit of talking about Jesus Christ as though 'Jesus' were His first name and 'Christ' were His surname. If He were to be given a surname it would probably be Bar-Joseph. 'Bar' means 'son of' and was often used to distinguish people from others who had the same first name. So Barabbas was probably the son of Abbas.

'Christ' is actually a word which was used for someone who had been anointed for a special purpose. In the early days, the Priests were anointed for their special job of providing a contact between God and human beings.

Later, the Kings were thought of as being specially selected by God to do God's work as rulers of the people, and so they too were the 'anointed ones'. The word 'Christ' would, therefore, apply to Priests and Kings, or anyone anointed for the work of leading people in the direction intended by God.

After the death of Moses, The Israelites felt that they needed another great leader or 'anointed one' to save them from their difficulties, and they thought that they had found such a leader in their Kings, especially King David.

But that also proved to be just a passing phase, and they were soon wishing for another 'Christ' to restore their greatness and success, as Moses and King David had done.

They talked about **The** Christ, the special anointed one who was to bring this about.

When Jesus came on the scene, many people thought of Him as the new 'Christ', but He was not at all keen to be thought of as 'the Christ', because that suggested political leadership - kicking out the Roman invaders and restoring success and prosperity to the Jewish nation, which was not at all what Jesus came to do.

After the death of Jesus, His followers realised that He had in fact brought a new and successful way of life to all who accept Him. So they used the word 'Christ' in a new way, not to denote a political anointed leader to restore good fortune, but to denote a person who was set apart by God to save all of us from getting our lives totally out of true. So when we use the word 'Christ' to speak about Jesus, we accept that He was actually set apart by God to ensure that, if we respond to Him, our life will be kept on the right path.

*This prayer, like all prayers, ends with the word '**Amen**'.*
Amen.

We get so used to rattling off this word after every prayer, that we can easily stop thinking what we are saying.

It is a Hebrew word which means 'to prop up' or 'to show firmness'. The word 'firm' or 'secure' or 'sure' came to be used in the same way as the Americans use the word 'Sure!' – to show agreement with what has been said, or af**firm** it. The Jews finished prayers with it to show that they agreed with the words which had been said, also that they had firm faith that the promises made by God would be fulfilled.

In private prayer, it says "I mean that, and I trust you, God". So we end a prayer with 'Amen' to show our agreement with what has been said, and to express our confidence in God.

We have now completed our understanding of the words at the beginning of the service, and already we see that they are not just words to be repeated thoughtlessly each week, but that they have a deep and important meaning, which will affect our whole attitude to what is going to follow.

The service may now remind us of God's **Commandments.**
The Commandments.

God did not dream up a lot of rules just to make our life difficult. The Commandments show us how to behave if we want to fit in successfully with the way the world is made.

In the history of the different religions of man, there are many long books of laws about how people should behave towards God and to each other. But the ten commandments manage to sum it all up in very short sentences.

They were, like some of the other sets of laws, written on tablets of stone. Paper and parchment were not regarded as long-lasting enough for such precious documents.

The ten commandments were then kept in a special 'ark' (or safe box) by the Israelites, and taken around with them everywhere they went.

Jesus later summed up the commandments in even shorter words because, basically, they tell us to love God and to want the best for the other people around us.

It is right that we should be reminded of the commandments at the start of a service, while our minds are being opened to think about God, and what God wants us to do.

Lord have **mercy**.....
Mercy.

Its underlying meaning is 'kindness', - with or without love.Then it came to mean **behaving** in a kindly way, including kindness to people who may deserve punishment. So when we say 'Lord have mercy', we are asking God to treat us kindly. Of course, there may be some difference between our idea of kindness and what God knows is kind.

A parent may not, for example, always be kind to let the bad behaviour of a child go unchecked, a fact which the child may not quite appreciate!

Fred and Rex seemed not to share the same ideas about kindness when it came to winter walks!

In some versions of the service we next say our confession. In others it is left until later, but associated with it are.....
The **Comfortable** *Words.*

Comfortable.

These days we think of 'comfortable' as something physical, like a nice easy chair or a bed in which we are relaxed. But the same idea can apply to our state of mind, and this is how the word is used here. These words spoken by Jesus are intended to help us to feel more at ease, so that we are not feeling 'uncomfortable' for the rest of our life because of the things which we have done wrong.

The word 'comfort' is from two Latin words which mean 'together' and 'strong'. When God is together with us, we are strong. The 'Comfortable Words' remind us that God does not just abandon us if we are ready to start afresh.

.....gave His only Son, **Jesus** *Christ.....*

Jesus.

We have seen how the Jews saw the importance of a **name.**
The name 'Jesus' is the same word as 'Joshua' or 'Jeshua', and means 'God saves'.

This is why at Christmas we read how Joseph was told...
"You shall call His name Jesus, for He shall **save** His people from their sins."

.....gave His only **Son***, Jesus Christ.....*

Son.

The word has two ideas attached to it.

1. Obviously, the son is a part of the parents, and he has in him many of their genes and characteristics. This is why the family has always been an important unit. In Hebrew, the word '**son of**' means 'having the character of' or 'belonging to the group of'.

Our children are all
so very much like
their daddy . . .

2. In Jewish families, a son was more important than a daughter. This is hard for us to understand in our non-sexist society, but that was the way in which they thought. The reason for this was that their family name was continued through the males - and family was a most important feature of Jewish social life. Therefore, the possessions of the family were given to the sons in order of seniority.

Whilst on the subject of sons, we might as well look at two special ways in which the word 'son' has been used.

Son of God.

Following the meanings of 'son' we have just considered, to be called a '**son of God**' meant that you had many of God's characteristics and that you had God's special favour.

Various people in the Old Testament were called sons of God. So was Jesus.

An extra complication is that the term 'Son of God' was used by Jewish people to talk about the person who was said to be coming to save the Jewish nation, the Messiah.

The Jews expected a great **Messiah**, whom they thought of as being a very powerful person, who would crush God's enemies and establish the Jewish race as the most important on earth. And that is how some people thought of Jesus. That is why Jesus told His disciples not to call Him 'Messiah'. (*See also under the word '**Christ**'.*)

So we see that, linked up with remarks about being the 'Son of God', are the ideas of (a) being part of God, (b) being the one who has special favour with God, and (c) being the one who is to save people. (*See also under the word '**save**'.*)

15

*.....gave His **only** Son, Jesus Christ.....*
Only.

So why was Jesus called the 'only' son, especially if other people had also been called 'son of God'?

Christians believe that Jesus is the **only** person who actually had the perfect attributes of 'a son of God', being the same as God, on whom God's favour rests, and who is able to be our Saviour. That is why we call Him the **'only'** son of God.

Which leads us on to the other special use of the word 'son'.
Son of Man.

This was used of people who had all the best characteristics of a human being.

In the book of Daniel it was used to represent a special man who would come in the future to inspire people to live in the way in which God wishes - to let our lives be ruled by God instead of by all the wrong ways in which man usually chooses to live. Jesus used 'Son of Man' to describe Himself because it gave a better picture of what He was doing than did 'Son of God', (which, as we have seen, contained the idea of a Messiah).

So this is why 'Son of Man' is also used to describe Jesus.

If we understand it in this way, there is no contradiction in calling Jesus either the 'Son of God' or the 'Son of Man', because He had the characteristics implied in either of those descriptions.

The Minister invites us to say our confession.....
.....in **faith**.....

Faith.

People use this word in different ways. For some it means believing in the impossible. For some it means trust.
For some it means belief in God.
In the Bible, it comes from a word which has to do with 'strength' and 'firmness'.
The easiest picture to show the difference between belief and faith is the old one of the man crossing Niagara Falls on a tight-rope, wheeling a wheelbarrow.
You may believe he can do it, but '**faith**' is when your belief is so strong that you are prepared to let him take **you** across in the wheelbarrow!

We may claim that we believe in God, but when it comes to the moment of decision, are we really prepared to accept the practical consequences of what we say we believe?

The word 'faith' is also used in another way.
The Faith (with a big F) is sometimes used by people to refer to their own favourite version of religion.

Old Mr and Mrs Brown displayed great faith in accepting a lift to church from Bill each Sunday.

This is a bit confusing, because the word '**religion**' basically means 'being tied to something', 'devoutness' or 'reverence'.
It then came to mean any particular system of beliefs - such as Hinduism or Buddhism or Christianity.
So 'religion' is not the same as 'faith', even if a religion does need people who have faith.

It is with **penitence** *and faith that we say our Confession.*
Penitence.
'Penitence' is a noun made from the verb to '**repent**', (*and is explained under that heading*). If 'repentance' is willingness to turn away from doing wrong, 'penitence' suggests not only turning away but also being ready to <u>make amends</u> for the wrong which has been done.

In our Confession, we admit that we don't always get things right, and sometimes deliberately do wrong.
We say with **penitence** that we are ready to do something about it, having complete **faith** that God will not hold our past mistakes against us.
God allows us to make a fresh start, so that we need not go around feeling guilty and unforgiven for things which we, or other people, have done in the past.
(*See also under the word* **'Forgive'**)

The Confession.
The Confession follows naturally at this point in the service.
We have thought about what God wants us to do.
We know that.....
we have sometimes done wrong on purpose (our **sins**),
we have sometimes done wrong by mistake (our **errors**)
and, of course, there were times when we didn't bother to do good, because we were too lazy, too easily distracted, or just because we wanted to avoid argument (our **negligence**).
So it is to God that we now admit, or confess, these failings.

There are several possible forms of confession. We now look at some of the words most commonly found in confessions.

Confess.

The actual word to 'confess' is a bit like the word to 'admit', and is used by us in two slightly different ways.

1. If we 'confess' belief in something, we admit openly that we believe in it. So people 'confessed God', meaning that they admitted that God existed.

2. It also means 'to admit' in the sense of saying that we have made a mistake, or done wrong.

So we 'confess **to** God' where we have gone wrong. This is the way in which the word is used in our services when we say our 'Confession'.

We have **sinned**.....

To 'sin' is to commit one sin or more. So let's see what is ....

A sin.

The word 'sin' has many different shades of meaning, which depend on who is using it.

Basically, 'sin' is any behaviour which goes contrary to that which God tells us is right. In some parts of the Bible it is limited to <u>deliberately</u> wrong behaviour, in others it includes wrong behaviour done by ignorance or mistake.

If God says you must not kill and you deliberately kill, you have sinned.

What if you wish your enemy would fall down a deep hole? Jesus tells us, in some fairly tough talking, that this is just as much of a sin as actually killing your enemy. He says that if you wish harm to someone, your thoughts can be just as deliberate a disobedience of God's commands as when you actually do the harm itself.

So what if I deliberately kick the football at the referee, and pretend it was a mistake? Surely that is just 'naughty', it isn't sin is it?

Yes, it is sin. If you deliberately cause any unpleasantness, either inside yourself or to other people, it is totally against God's principle. So it ranks as sin just as much.

'Naughtiness' is a word which people use to make sin seem less important - just as 'it fell off a lorry' may mean 'I stole it'. There is no such thing as a 'little' sin, or a 'little' theft. All theft involves the same mental attitude whatever is taken. **Anything done deliberately, knowing it is wrong, is sin.**

This leaves us with things done wrong, but **not** deliberately. Although at times the Bible confuses it, we ought to make a distinction between deliberate and non-deliberate sin. If we do something wrong by mistake, it is really 'error'.

.....*through* **negligence**.....

Negligence.

If you 'neglect' to do something, the word suggests that you just did not try to do anything about it. Allowing wrong to take place, when you know perfectly well that it **is** wrong but can't be bothered to stop it, counts under the heading of sin.

There were times when Bill's ability to be distracted amounted to sheer negiligence.

.....*through* **weakness**.....

Weakness.

We have just seen that if you know that someone is doing wrong, and you don't stop them, it is negligence. By your neglect to do anything, you are really committing a sin too. You may, however, try to suggest to them a better way but find that they are stronger than you and persist in doing it anyway. You could not be called sinful for being too weak to stop them. So that sort of weakness is not sinful.

But there is also another kind of weakness, where you are too weak and weedy to stop **yourself** from deliberately doing wrong. Unless you are so handicapped that you are regularly unable to control what you do, your weakness of character is no excuse, just as being drunk is no excuse for doing wrong either! You still deliberately did wrong, and that is sin. Had you been more strong-minded, or less drunk, you might have stopped it.

.....through **ignorance.....**

Ignorance.

There is another version of the confession which contains the admission that we have sinned through ignorance. This is another of those words which have two meanings.

Sometimes it means 'not knowing'. It is hard to see how we can commit a sin (as opposed to 'error') if we do not know we are doing wrong.

But ignorance is also connected with the word 'ignore'.

If you 'ignore' something, you deliberately refuse to notice it. We cannot use that sort of ignorance as a good excuse for doing wrong.

In other words, if we have never heard of Jesus, or have never been told how important His ideas are, we cannot be blamed for doing something which He has said is wrong.

If, on the other hand, we know He tells us the truth and then refuse to find out what things He **has** said, we have nobody but ourselves to blame if we go wrong.

.....we **repent**.....

Repent.

Many people think that to 'repent' is the same as to say 'I am sorry'. It isn't. The true meaning behind this word is 'to turn round and go in a different direction'.

Which is why we say we are sorry **and** say that we repent. If you are not even sorry, you will probably not see the need to turn round and go in a different direction in future.

But it is quite easy to **say** you are sorry and still not bother to turn round and go in a different direction in future.

You can say you are sorry till the cows come home, but if you don't repent, you might as well sing "We are poor little lambs who have gone astray, baa, baa, baa..... who cares?"

'I'm sorry' is often used as a way of getting out of trouble, or escaping someone's anger, and it may have nothing to do with repentance at all.

So our confession is much more than a lip-service by which we admit that we have done wrong. It is promise that we will turn round and go in a different direction next time, and so in future deliberately avoid that wrong behaviour.

After our Confession, God offers us **absolution**.

Absolution, absolve.

Anything with 'solve' in it has a meaning of loosening something or letting it come apart. And 'ab' means 'away'. So God allows our sins to come away from us, rather like a scab falls away from a wound, showing the good clean flesh underneath. (*See below, under the word* '***Forgive***')

Most of the forms of absolution contain the word.....

Forgive, or forgiveness

Some people seem to think that 'forgiveness' is just saying "Oh, that's all right, it doesn't really matter", when wrong is done to us or to others. Such an idea is not at all helpful, - of course it matters. It matters a lot to all concerned.

Nor does it mean escaping punishment. It and forgiveness are not to be linked at all. (Why **do** we punish, actually?)

There are various meanings from which '**forgive**' has come,

1. 'to cover' or 'draw a veil over'
2. 'to pacify' or 'establish peace', and
3. 'to lift away' or 'to give away'.

These all help to give us a clue as to what forgiveness is.

First, we don't leave a wound exposed and raw, we cover it over and let it heal. So too we should let all our hurts heal.

Second, we don't keep on aggravating it, we give it peace.

Third, we finally let it lift away, as scabs finally lift away.

So when someone has done wrong we don't keep on yakking about it and reminding everyone of it, we let it rest.

This is not the same as 'forgetting' or trying to hide it.

It is not helpful, and may even be harmful, to shove hurts away to the back of the mind and try to 'forget' them.

But we do not keep on constantly irritating the wound.

Next, we establish peace; peace in ourself by not allowing ourself to continue to feel hurt and over-sensitive, and peace in those who did wrong, by letting them know that they do not have to be upset about it for ever.

Finally, we don't let the wrong fester for the rest of our life.

Hatred, resentment and anger do more damage to the person who cannot forgive than they do to the person who is hated.

Let the scab fall away, and make a fresh start.

We need to be able to 'give away' resentment and anger.

Remember, forgiveness is not 'forgetting' or saying the action is all right, it is just letting it heal for all concerned.

What if the wrong-doers won't accept this? It does not alter the fact that you have forgiven the situation, it just means that they have cut themselves off from the forgiveness, which is sad, because in that case, the healing can only be completed for you, not for them.

It also usually mentions..... '**life** *eternal*' *or* '*everlasting* **life***'.*
Life.

For most of us, the word 'life' means being physically alive. Sometimes we use it for 'liveliness' when we say someone is 'full of life', as opposed to being 'a dead loss'.

But 'life' is not as simple as that, because there are at least 9 different words used in the original Bible, all of which have been translated as the word 'life' in English! It would be fairly pointless to go into them all here, because this book is trying to be a straightforward help to the basic meaning of some of the words which we use in church. But it may be of interest to know that the different words include 'physical existence', 'breath', 'activity', 'number of days spent alive on earth', 'recovery from sickness', and 'to prosper'.

In modern Christianity, it has come to be associated with successful existence, whether of the body or the soul.

As we believe that our existence does not end when the body dies, our successful existence may well continue for ever in the presence of God, which is '**eternal**' life. This may sometimes be compared with unsuccessful existence, or separation from God, which by contrast is called '**death**'.

After Confession, we are assured that God will not hold our sins against us for ever, so that our eternal life need not be in danger at this point, provided that we do repent.

Granny gave a whole new meaning to 'eternal life' at the Praise Services.

At some point in the service we give **glory** *to God, using the words 'Glory to God in the highest', (The Latin for that is 'Gloria in excelsis'.) This is usually done after we have been promised absolution or after we have had our Communion.*

Glory *to God in the highest.....*
Glory.
This word is taken from several original words which mean
a) 'Honour', or 'the trappings of honour' (gold, posh clothes, bright and rich surroundings.) - 'Brightness' later took over.
b) The good opinion, or respect, which others have of you.
c) 'Weight', including the 'weight' of authority.
When we talk about the 'glory' of God, we mean all these.
In other words, we mean the honour and respect which God is given, the authority of God, and the 'brightness' of God's presence (*see also under* **'light'**). Glory **'to'** God means that we will offer **to** God's authority our honour and respect.

Glory to God in the **highest**.....
Highest.
Human minds have, perhaps unfortunately, always thought in terms of UP and DOWN, and tend to associate UP with good and DOWN with bad. A good pupil is TOP of the class.
We go UP in someone's estimation if we are good.
So we talk about going UP to God and DOWN to hell.
Even Jesus used the term 'ascend' when going to God, it was just a natural part of the vocabulary which people used.
It is rather a pity that we think like this, because it makes God seem to have a limited place 'up there'. But we are stuck with it - we just don't need to take it too literally.
This is added to because the earth is round, which means that, when you are standing anywhere on the earth, anything outside it must seem to be UP.

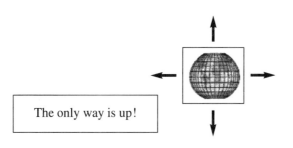

The only way is up!

.....**heavenly** *King*.....

Heaven.

Since we have just been talking about 'up' and 'down', we might as well think about the real meaning of Heaven, which quite a lot of people seem to think of as being 'somewhere **up** there'.

At one point in Jewish history, the word 'Heaven' was, like the word 'Lord', used to replace the name of 'God'. This was because, as we have already said, the Jews were not allowed to call God by name.

The word has associations with the idea of 'heaving' or 'lifting up'.

It has become a popular idea for two reasons.

First because of the association of perfection as being the HIGHEST thing, and second because we love to think in terms of everything having a place. It is hard to think of anything as just existing without it existing somewhere.

The idea of heaven covers both these needs, being 'above' (i.e. better than) us and being the 'place' where God exists.

It is just as unfortunate as using 'up' and 'down', because it gives a totally wrong impression of God. Here again, Jesus used the word because it was commonly used in Jewish understanding.

So this is another word with which we are lumbered, but which we don't need to take too literally, other than to show the goodness of God, and sharing in God's existence.

When we talk about people 'going to heaven', we need to remember that we mean they are going to share in God's existence, love and goodness.

So our 'heavenly King' refers to one who rules over us (King), who is good, and who has eternal existence.

.....we **worship** *You.....*

Worship.

This word has become associated with the official church Services. We talk about going to Divine Worship.

It really means 'giving value, (or worth), to'.

So when we 'worship' God, it means that we are recognising the true worth (or 'worth-ship') of God.

'Worship' is also a translation of some words which mean 'the service and respect given by servants to a master'.

One hopes that people do not go to church just to mumble through a lot of words, sing hymns which may or may not make sense, or to shake hands with a clergyman. Yet they sometimes say that they will stop going to church because they don't like the hymns, the words used, or the clergyman!

We go to church   **a) to value the WORTH of,**

        b) to learn more about,

      and c) to show respect and service to
            - GOD.

HOW we worship is less important than WHY we worship. If you stay away from regular public worship which you could attend, you refuse to admit to the world that God is worth much to you.

Whom do you worship?

27

.....**Lamb** *of God*.....
Lamb.
This must be a very confusing
word to people who have no
religious background. They
come into a church and hear
"Behold the Lamb of God!",
and there isn't a sheep in sight!
Back in ancient Jewish history,

I was lost and the lamb
showed me the way home!

it was customary to sacrifice, or set aside for God, the first
of everything which was given to you - the first ears of corn
from the field, the first oranges, or other fruit, from the trees
that year, the first new-born lamb, and even the first child.
(Some of the other so-called 'civilisations' in that area were
in the habit of sacrificing children to their gods anyway.)
But it didn't seem too sensible to kill your first child, so they
used a lamb as the sacrifice instead.
The lamb was used to **'redeem'** or 'pay' for the child's life.
Jesus chose to die rather than submit to evil and wrong.
If He had not died, there would have been no Christian religion, and we should still be living in many ways which were
totally wrong - miles away from the pattern which God
intends for us.
So, by dying, Jesus saved our lives in a way which was rather
like the lamb being killed to save the life of the child.
It may all seem a bit barbaric to us, who know that God does
not want lambs killed to represent the life of a child, or as
any form of sacrifice to God, but it was a very meaningful
picture to the Jews of the time of Jesus.
It can also be very meaningful to us, if we understand that
Jesus gave up His physical existence here on earth so that
you and I might have eternal life, (*which is explained under
the word 'Life'*). We therefore say 'Lamb of God' with great
reverence and gratitude.

.....**take away the sins** *of the world*.....
Take away our sins.
We often say that Jesus died 'for our sins', or 'to take away our sins'.

When you think of what we said about the Lamb of God, it becomes clear what this means.

Look at the way people are likely to behave when they do not know what Jesus told us. We get rulers who kill people left right and centre. We also get aggressive, selfish, cynical and unpleasant people all over the world. We may even get them among our regulars in church sometimes (presumably calling themselves 'Christian' before they have yet learned what Christ really intended us to be!).

So Jesus does **take away** from the world many wrong ways of doing things, if we are truly prepared to do as He tells us. He saves from sin and error all the individuals or nations that behave as He suggests. They will then have a much more sensible and fulfilled existence - here and now with God, and also with God in eternity.

There is, therefore, a striking similarity between the lamb being sacrificed in the olden days to redeem or save the life of a child, and Jesus sacrificing His life to save us from being cut off from God.

.....**seated** *at the right hand of God*.....

This idea is linked with the idea of a...

Throne.

The Jewish nation thought of its kings as representatives of God. If the kings had thrones, then God would also have a throne - a special place from which to make important official decisions and announcements. Which is why there are many passages of scripture in which God is pictured as sitting on a throne.

We know that this is a rather poor picture, because it limits God too much, but provided we understand that it represents God's authority and power, we can go along with it.

.....seated at the **right hand** *of God*.....

It has been a long-established custom for the important visitor to sit at the <u>right</u> of the host. We still talk of someone close to a person in authority as being his 'right-hand man'. We here continue that rather questionable throne picture, where Jesus is seen as God's 'right-hand man', for which the writer of the Book of Revelation must bear a lot of responsibility.

.....in the glory of God the **Father**.....

Father.

Jesus often speaks of God as His 'Father', and He taught us to call God our Father too.

It ties up with what we have said about the word **'son'**.

But the idea of being so familiar as to call God our 'Father' would be considered very 'cheeky' compared with the rather more formal and distant idea of God which the Jews had in their tradition. Especially as Jesus used a word like 'Daddy'.

We need to remember that the traditional Jewish father was a very important figure in the household. There was a deep family bond. But the father not only gave his inheritance to his children, he ruled them firmly and expected obedience and respect. This may be slightly different from some of the modern ideas of a father!

It may also be very difficult, or even painful, for people who have had bad fathers to have to think of God as a father at all. It might be equally meaningless for some people to try to speak of God as 'parent' these days.

It is not very helpful when people get so tied up with such 'picture' words that they object to God being a 'Father' and try to use the word 'Mother' instead. This really shows that they are thinking more of their own importance than that of God. Jesus used the word 'Father' because He wanted to get the Jews to see God in the proper way.

Basically, it marked a huge change away from thinking of God as remote and revengeful. Instead, we think of God as the one to whom we owe our existence, who cares for us and who is willing to share everything with us, who is ready to listen to us, and to whom we owe love, obedience and respect.

Does God love Teddy too!

*Part of the service may be headed '***The Word***'.*
It includes the Collect, readings, and words of explanation from the Minister. After a reading, the speaker may say.....
This is the **word** *of the Lord.*
Word.

This is another much misunderstood idea. In common talk, a 'word' is a group of letters which is given a meaning.

To say that the Collect, readings and sermon, are the 'Word' seems to suggest that the 'Word' is just spoken or read.

It is a mistake to think this.

In religious terms, the 'Word of God' is anything which reveals the meaning or person of God.

So creation itself is the 'Word of God', because it shows us a lot about God.

The Bible is the 'Word of God', not just because it contains written words, but because it shows us something of what God is like.

Jesus is the 'Word of God'. He shows us more about God than anything or anyone else has done.

Do they really mean that?

> **DON'T LET WORRY KILL YOU, THE CHURCH CAN HELP**

> **DANGER! CHILDREN ROUND THE BEND**

They'd be furious if you did!

> **CAUTION CHILDREN**

> **WET FLOOR**

> **STOP CHILDREN CROSSING**

Confession time?

> **POLICE SLOW**

> **CROSS TRAFFIC AHEAD**

> **BUY HERE! DIRT CHEAP**

The <u>Human</u> word can be misinterpreted. How do we understand God's word?

As Jesus was a human being, in the flesh, St. John speaks of Jesus as 'The Word made flesh'.

So when we hear 'This is the word of the Lord', it means 'This is one of the ways in which God is shown to us'.

The **Collect**.

The special prayer associated with a particular day is called the 'Collect' for the day. It was originally supposed to collect together into one prayer the different ideas of the people assembled, and to sum up the 'theme' for the day.

It usually follows a set pattern. We call on God, we ask for something, and we admit the power of God. Some of the Collects go back into the very early days, and some have been made up more recently.

The **Gospel**.

The word 'Gospel' means 'glad tidings', or 'good news'.

In the Jewish, and later in the Christian, religion it meant the good news that God cares about us.

When Jesus talked about the 'good news' it usually meant that He was here to tell us that, anywhere where God's way was allowed to prosper, the world was 'good'.

With later writers, it became the idea that God saved people from spoiling their life and the world.

So the good news, now as much as then, is that God cares and can keep you and me right.

To complete our thinking at this point, we ought to work out what the word 'good' really means.

Good.

Some people talk about being 'good' as though it meant, behaving in a nice way or having a little halo. Which it does not really mean.

It was originally translated in the Bible from a word which meant that something was pleasing, such as the 'good' news we have just been thinking about.

In English, the word 'good' really means 'doing properly that for which it was made'. A vacuum-cleaner is made to pick up dust, so a 'good' vacuum-cleaner is one which picks up dust properly.

Fruit is meant to be eaten, or so we think. We therefore call a 'good' apple one which is nice to eat. If it is going brown and is not nice to eat we say it is a 'bad' apple.

We may not always agree about what something is made for, in which case we shall differ about what we call 'good'.

And God may have other ideas about why something was made. Fruit was actually made in the first place to spread seed and produce more fruit. So an apple which is brown and rotting to allow the seed to go into the ground may be seen as 'good' in God's eyes.

Jesus told us how to live in the way for which God created us. And so people who follow His ways are 'good' in the proper meaning of the word.

During the service, we may be invited to say **the Creed.**
Creed.

The word comes from the Latin 'credo' meaning 'I believe'. In the early days, if someone joined the Christian church, that person was expected to make a general statement of what he or she believed. There were two versions.

The Nicene Creed was used in the Eastern countries, and the Apostles Creed was used in the Western countries.

We have kept both versions in our modern church.

At one time, the Creed was a very solemn part of the service, and there are still people who don't feel that we do right if we leave it out or modernise it.

Whilst it may be useful for people to say what they believe, we must remember that Jesus did not have such 'passports' for His followers, and it raises the question as to whether He would actually approve of it. On that, people may differ.

We use both versions of the Creed as we now look at the words which are to be found in them.

We believe in **one God**.....

In the days before the Jews, it was customary to worship many different Gods. Then people began to believe in one God, who was the creator of everything.

Jesus talked about the creative power of God as being like that of a father, (*which we have talked about elsewhere*).

Jesus also talked about the Holy Spirit, which was to come upon His followers after He had returned to the Father.

So people now had three descriptions of God. God who created everything, God as revealed in Jesus, and then there was the Holy Spirit. It seemed a bit confusing. Were there three Gods - the Creator, Jesus and the Holy Spirit?

The creed, therefore, deliberately began with a belief in **one** God to remind us that, although Jesus and the Holy Spirit may be aspects of God, they are all part of the one creator.

We have already talked about the Father, who is the 'maker of heaven and earth'. (See **'Lord'**)

.....**all that is, seen and unseen**.....

Remember to put the break at the comma. 'All that is', means 'everything in existence'.

It does not mean 'all <u>that is seen</u> and unseen'. That may add up to the same, but without the comma, does not really make sense as English! In the other version, it says, 'All things visible and invisible'. Even this would make more sense with a comma, i.e. all things, visible and invisible.

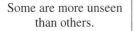

Some are more unseen than others.

35

.....eternally begotten *of the Father....(or before all worlds)*
'Begotten'

This is a longer word for 'owing its existence to'. Remember that this creed was put together at a conference of bishops in Nicea, more than 300 years after Jesus had been crucified. Not all creeds use the words 'eternally begotten'. So how can we say that Jesus 'eternally' owes His existence to God? It was not only when Jesus appeared on the scene that people began to behave in the way in which He taught us.

They had from earliest times been doing many of the things which He tells us are right. So, in that sense, some of the ideas of Jesus, being the ideas of God, had been around since the beginning of time. But it was in Jesus that they all came together to make complete sense in one human life.

This is one way in which the idea can be explained.

Other people see it as meaning that Jesus existed from the same time as God existed. This is in some sense true, because in God we also have all the characteristics of Jesus already in existence.

The next words seem to underline this.

.....God from God..... (God of God)

These words were put in to show the truth of the previous idea. Jesus was part of the plan by which God was to be shown to people on this earth.

Jesus came from God and is actually God being shown to us in a way which is practical and clear for human beings to understand.

In the version which says 'God of God' the word **'of'**, rather than meaning 'belonging to', means 'from' as when we say something was done 'of necessity'.

.....**Light from light**.....(Light of Light)

Darkness and light are important in all human life.

People have always felt insecure in darkness, because we cannot see clearly what is happening around us.

If we try to move about in complete darkness, we bump into things and hurt ourselves.

So it is not surprising that the ideas of darkness and light have continued to be used when talking about our mind and our way of living. We talk about 'keeping someone in the dark' when we don't let them know what is happening. We say that we are 'in the dark' if we don't understand something, and we ask to be 'enlightened'.

It is, therefore, only natural that the same words were used in the same way in religious language too. So we talk about 'the light of God's truth' and we call Jesus 'the light of the world' because He showed us clearly what life should be like.

Once we know about life as Jesus explains it, we have all the 'light' which prevents us from blundering about and hurting ourself and doing damage to other people. It is not surprising that Jesus should, therefore, be called 'the light of the world'.

So Jesus was inspired by the 'light' of God's truth, and at the same time He **was** that truth in His own life.

In this sense He **is** light which **came** from light.

Don't go running off, lunch is nearly ready.

You can't get lost near a lighthouse!

.....**true God from true God**.....('very God of very God')
The newer version gives the better sense than the older.
In the older version, 'very' was a word which came from the
Latin 'verus' connected with the idea of 'truth' ('veritas').
It is in our word 'to verify' or 'prove the truth of something'.
Obviously, these words in the creed are just underlining the
previous idea, namely, 'God from God, Light from Light'.
It was not in the original version but became added later.
The writers probably thought it gave greater emphasis to say
it three times. As we have seen, God is thought of as Father,
Son and Holy Spirit, and it may have influenced them to put
the three parts to this picture of Jesus. It shows Jesus as of
the Father/Creator, bringing Light to Humans, and also the
true Spirit of God.

.....**begotten, not made**.....
This is a very careful use of words.
To 'beget' means 'to be the source from which something
exists'. Such as when we say, cruelty 'begets' more cruelty.
To 'make', means to 'create', 'construct' or 'manufacture'
something.
We 'make' a noise, because we create it ourselves.
We 'make' a nuisance of ourselves, because our behaviour
creates a situation which annoys other people.
So the writers of this creed are stressing that God was the
source from which Jesus came, not that God actually 'made'
or 'manufactured' Jesus. - A bit deep, that. Come back to it
when you are more into studying theology!

.....**of one Being** *with the Father*......(of one substance with)
The verb 'to be' just means 'to exist'. It has no picture of shape or size, it does not even convey any idea of activity or thought.

In the Old Testament, God is described as 'I AM'.

This is a good description because it stops people making pictures of God - how can you picture 'I exist'?

It is not past or future either, just existence.

From this we get the idea of a '**being**', meaning something which exists.

A 'human being' is something which exists in human shape, but doesn't describe any particular shape, thought or activity other than 'being' human.

The writers of this creed were very keen that people should not think of Jesus as being separate in identity from God. Jesus is one existence with God, i.e. 'of one being' with God. Put in human terms, your spirit and your body are an equal part of your existence. Your body and your spirit cannot be separated, otherwise **you** do not exist.

So your body and your spirit are 'of one being' with you.

Without God, Jesus would not have existed either, because there would have been no point in Him coming to show us about a God who did not exist! So they really are of one 'being', inseparable.

'Of one **substance**' is an old-fashioned use of 'substance'. It does not mean solid matter. It is a poor translation of the original Greek in which the creed was written. The original word was more like 'basic nature' or 'essence'. So that Jesus was being described as having the same basic nature as God. It was like the word 'property' when used in the sense that a gas has certain 'properties', meaning basic characteristics.

.....and for **our salvation.....**
Salvation, Saviour.
The word 'to save' is used a lot in our worship.
The act of saving is called 'salvation', the person who does the saving is the 'saviour'. It has three basic meanings.
1. **To keep safe**, as when we 'save' our money in a bank. The Jews often called God their 'Saviour' when they said that God had given them victory in battle and so had saved their nation from extinction, to be of use in future.
2. **To keep successfully alive.** Jesus prevents us from many errors which ruin our life.
3. **To snatch away from danger**, as when a brave fireman snatches you away from flames.

These ideas are all mixed together when we say that God or Jesus is our 'Saviour', or the means of our 'Salvation'. Because.....
God and Jesus keep us safe and successfully alive, (not only alive in our body, but in our personality too.).
They also snatch us away from a very serious danger.
The danger from which they save us is that of behaving in such a way as to cause trouble for ourself and other people, and so, finally, we are saved from losing touch with God.
Of course, we need to accept what they have to offer, and to actually turn away from all that would harm and hurt us. (*We have already seen this under 'repentance'.*)
That is why the ideas of 'repentance' and 'salvation' go very closely together.

.....the **quick** and the dead.....
There is an old joke that on our modern roads there are only two kinds of pedestrians - the quick, and the dead.
But in the Creed, the word 'quick' does not mean 'moving rapidly'. It is an old-fashioned word for 'alive.'

.....his **Kingdom** *will have no end.*
Kingdom.
The real meaning of the 'kingdom' is the place where a ruler is allowed to rule.
So the kingdom of God is anywhere where God's way is allowed to flourish..
People sometimes think of it as one definite place, which is the **wrong** idea of God's kingdom.
Jesus said to us that 'The kingdom of God is within you'.
If you live as God wants you to, the **king**dom of God **is** within you, for that is where God is being allowed to rule.
Even the disciples misunderstood and said
"When you come into your kingdom......" thinking either that Jesus was going to throw out the Romans and become King of that region, or that Jesus was going to a special place where He would rule. It makes much more sense if we think of the 'kingdom of God' as anywhere where God is allowed to rule, including your own house or family or friends.
In this sense, the rule of God will never end, even if many places may reject that rule for a while.

He has spoken through the **prophets**.
Prophet.
In everyday language a 'prophet' is 'someone who foretells the future.' That is not what it means in the language of the Bible. In the Bible, it means someone who speaks to us on behalf of God. Obviously, if the prophet sees an important truth, it might well show us what will happen if we continue as we are doing now. After all, if you see someone running towards a cliff edge you may be able to see that, unless they turn around, they will suffer damage!

Prophets are sometimes rather unpopular, because they have to tell people a truth which those people do not want to hear. It is much nicer for the prophet when he can tell the people that God is pleased with the way they are going on.

In this creed we say we believe that the prophets whom we read about in the Bible were inspired by God.

......one holy **catholic and apostolic** *church.....*

Apostolic

This means 'in an unbroken line from the apostles of Jesus'. (We use the word apostle for the first followers of Jesus and later for the first Christian missionary to a country. The word just means 'a messenger'.)

Catholic.

This does not mean 'Roman Catholic', as some people seem to think.

When we talk about someone having a 'catholic' taste, it means that the person accepts a wide variety of experiences. This is the real meaning of that word.

So the 'catholic' church means all the wide variety of ways in which Christian churches worship, and the different ideas which they have. They may behave differently, and in some ways think differently, but they are all ONE church because they get their inspiration from the life, thoughts and spirit of Jesus.

We worship in our different ways
But it's One God who gets the praise.

After the prayers we may say something with the words.....
.....for the **sake** of..... *Jesus*
Sake
This is a strange word. It comes originally from the German word 'Sache', meaning 'business' / 'affair' / 'cause'.
In English it has come to mean the **cause** for which something is done.
'He lost all his money for the sake of a single mistake'.
(The mistake caused his loss)
'Please don't tell anyone, for my sake'.
(I am the cause of you keeping quiet about it.)
So when we pray something 'for the sake of Jesus' we are saying that Jesus is the **cause** of our prayer. It is another way of saying that our prayer is not being done just because **we** want it that way, but because we think that Jesus would want it that way.
In other words, it prevents our prayers from being done for entirely selfish motives.

.....**through** Jesus Christ.....
Through.
This really has the same effect as that which we have just said about 'for the sake of'.
There are people who think we should not approach God with our own ideas but should direct them to Jesus,who will then 'pass them on' to God!
Such thinking suggests two wrong things. First, that God and Jesus are not the same thing, which is not very sensible. Second, that God is not approachable by us directly, which contradicts all that Jesus told us anyway!
Praying 'through' Jesus means we are doing a quick check to see that we are not thinking in a purely selfish way, but that Jesus would approve of what we are trying to say.

*In many services today we say that we hope that God's **Peace** will be felt by those present.*

The Peace.

'Peace' in Christian terms is not just an absence of conflict, it is a gentleness of spirit which invades our whole person. It brings confidence, hope and a sense of proportion.

As long as the world around us refuses to accept the peace of God, we shall live in a constant state of conflict, so in that sense we cannot find perfect peace on earth.

But we do know that there is a tremendous sense of peace which comes to those who try to live in the same way as Jesus. It is that peace which we wish for one another.

At some point in every Communion service there is a special prayer, during which the everyday objects of bread, wine and water are set aside for a special purpose.
*It is called the Prayer of **Consecration.***

Consecration.

This word means setting something aside for a special purpose. In religion it usually means setting something aside specially for God. So when we 'consecrate' the ordinary bread and wine, they become set aside especially for God.

*Another word for this prayer is the **Eucharistic** Prayer, and some people call the whole service **'The Eucharist'***

Eucharist.

This is a Greek word which simply means 'thanksgiving'. (Actually it is a mixture of 'eu' which means 'beneficial', and 'charis' which means 'a free gift'. You probably are **thankful** if someone gives you a beneficial free gift!)

The word is used for the Communion service because it is reported that before Jesus broke the bread He **gave thanks** to God.

*Another word for the service is the **Holy Communion**.*
Communion.
The word really means 'sharing'. It is a good word to use for
a service in which each of us shares individually in the life
of Jesus, and where we all share in it together too.
(*'Holy' we have already explained*)

While on the subject, another word for the same service is
'The Mass'
Mass.
The word comes from the Latin word 'missio', which means
'I send'. After worship, the people were **sent out** to live and
work for God.

*The service is **Celebrated** by the person who takes it.*
Celebrate.
These days, to 'celebrate' means to have a good time on
some special occasion. Originally it was more concerned
with keeping a festival. The officiating priest is therefore
called the 'Celebrant'. It is he who says the prayer of
consecration.

Church Notice

While our vicar is away
the local clergy will be
celebrating with us.

During the prayer of Consecration, the following words are always said.

.....this is my **body**.....

We have to tackle this idea sooner or later. It has caused more emotion and discussion than practically any other word in our services. There are many different views of what we mean when we say that the bread at communion is the 'body' or 'flesh' of Jesus. Are we pretending to be cannibals?

It all comes about because of the words Jesus is reported as saying when He took His last meal with His disciples.

This last meal was to celebrate the old Jewish feast of the passover, when they ate unleavened bread, just as the Jews had done in Egypt before they were rescued by God from their slavery. So the bread was seen as an important part of the ceremony. **Unleavened** means without yeast in it. Many churches use a wafer which is made without yeast in it. At one point in the ceremony, Jesus took the bread, broke it, and said

"Take and eat this. This is my body, broken/given for you."

So let's be reasonable. We follow Jesus because He spoke sensibly about how to live.

He is not the sort of person to suggest that we should go through some strange cannibalistic ceremony in His honour. Jesus knew that He was on a collision course with the authorities, and that He was going to have to die in order to establish God's truth for human beings for ever.

He was indeed about to give his body for the sake of all the people who lived after Him, including us.

He has just washed the feet of His disciples as a last act to show that the whole point of His life was to teach us to want the best for others, rather than for ourselves, and to be willing to be of service to others, even if it meant doing quite humble tasks.

In a way which they will remember, He is now trying to show them that He is going to give up His body for their sake. And He asks them to remember this in future every time that they break bread together.

So naturally we do as He asks. We break bread in memory of that sacrifice He made.

The broken bread does indeed represent His broken body.

Each time we take it with true respect for what Jesus did for us, it does for us what His original sacrifice did for us all. In that sense, it is His body given for us all over again.

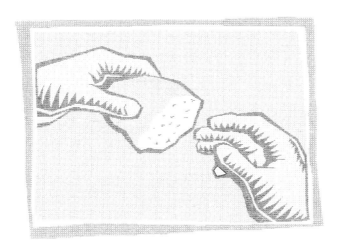

Body.

Unfortunately, the word 'body' is also used in the common way to mean 'a group of people', as in 'A fine body of men!'

So, 'We are the body of Christ' has two meanings.

We are the 'body' or group of people who are being Christ to the world.

We act as the physical appearance, or 'body', of Christ.

.....this is my **blood**.....

Blood.

Having got so far in understanding the body, we can more easily understand the meaning of His blood. It is being used in the same way as had just been explained with the bread. So why bother with the blood? Surely the bread would have been enough?

Jesus was a good teacher. He really wanted the message to get across, so the repetition was of use just for that purpose. But also, from earliest times, the blood has been a symbol of the whole life force. It represents not just our physical, or bodily, existence but our whole life, including the spirit.

That is why the Jewish priests offered sacrifices to God which included the body **and the blood** of the animal, a practice which was later proved unnecessary, but which all Jews knew about and respected.

So in telling them that the wine was His blood, Jesus was making it quite clear that it was not just His body which He was giving for them, but all that made up His life, including His spirit.

Each time we take it with true respect for what Jesus did for us, it does for us what His original sacrifice did for us all.

In that sense, it is His blood, His whole life force, shed for us once again.

To take our communion, therefore, is to be **renewed** with the whole life of Jesus. Not something to be done lightly or without due respect.

48

Some of the following words may also come into the prayer of Consecration.

.... therefore with **angels** *and archangels.....*

(*or there is other mention of angels*)

Angel.

The idea of angels does put some people off religion.

The word 'angel' simply means 'a messenger from God'.

So anyone is an angel who tells us something which God wants us to know.

Unfortunately, the whole idea has got clothed with pretty pictures of things flapping about with wings.

Some of the early writers, when they tried to picture what might happen at the end of the world, have been particularly good at drawing some way-out pictures - such as winged angels, seas of glass, many-headed beasts etc. All good symbolic fun but a bit off-putting until you understand what they are getting at. The Church seems to have latched on to this picture and started having angels floating around all over the place, having great armies and even ranks of angels, such as **archangels**, led by Michael, the **Seraphim** who were great on their zeal, and **Cherubim** who were the brainy ones and knew a lot!

We can be sure that there **are** angels in the sense that, in all ages, there are ways in which God manages to get messages across to us. We are told of two people dressed in white

 (no mention of wings!) whom Mary saw at the tomb of Jesus. How far we find the symbolic pictures helpful, however, will depend on each individual person. There is no need to let them put us off a religion which actually helps to put our whole life right.

Which is why we say a prayer which we call 'The Prayer of Humble Access', (or we use another similar one).
.....we do not come trusting in our own **righteousness**.....

Righteousness.

A much misunderstood word. In everyday speech, the word 'righteous' has come to mean a rather smug, self-satisfied sense that we are always right.

This is far from the real meaning as used in true religion.

'Righteousness' is the fact of **being** right, not the fact that you are **sure** you are right - and there is a great difference between those two things.

God is 'righteous' because what God does is right for all creation.

Jesus is 'righteous' because the way in which He lived, and all that He tells us, is right for all people everywhere.

So what we are saying here is that we are not presuming to come to God trusting that we are always doing what is right, but because we know that God is able to put us right when we go wrong.

In some of our services we say the Lord's Prayer before we share in the bread and wine, in others we say it immediately afterwards. In either case, it is right that, as we come closer to Jesus, we use the prayer which He taught us.

The Lord's Prayer.

First, we should realise that this is not just a jumble of words for us to repeat at given intervals when a button is pressed as though we were a mechanical toy.

That is not what Jesus intended.

It is a basic way of thinking when we pray to God.

1. Respect for our creator.
2. The hope that God's way will finally win on this earth.
3. We ask for help with the problems of our everyday life.
4. An understanding that we don't always do much to help bring about all the things for which we have prayed so far, so we might try a bit harder, and hope God will forgive us for our failings.
5. We realise that, if God is ready to forgive us, we need to be ready to forgive people who have done wrong to us.
6. The hope that we shall not find ourself tempted beyond our powers, and that, when temptation does come, God will help us not be spoiled by it, nor to fall from the right way.

We finish with an extra bit which Jesus did not say, but may still be useful, namely...

I know You can do it, God, and we should always respect You for it.

We don't have to use the same words each time when we pray like this, because we have different needs, and different hopes and fears as situations change, and as we change too. So we use our own words in the right pattern.

But we do actually repeat those words of Jesus sometimes, because they are a constant reminder of HOW we should pray, and not WHAT we should pray.

.....deliver us from **evil**.....

evil

Evil is not exactly the opposite of 'good'. 'Bad' is the word which shows the opposite of 'good'. A bad vacuum-cleaner does not pick up dust properly, and so is not doing that for which it was originally made. But we could not call it evil. The word 'evil' in the Bible is a translation of an old Hebrew word meaning 'to spoil' or 'to break into pieces', which suggests that the damage is being done on purpose.

At one point in the development of the world, a species came along which could actually think and make decisions. At that point there was a chance to make a decision to follow the pattern of creation, or deliberately to damage it. Free-will had arrived. Presumably, God could have done away with all free-will by making humans become extinct. In which case the world would have remained static, and there would have been no further possible development. We must, therefore, assume that creatures with free-will are actually part of the development pattern created by God.

This really gets rid of that rather futile question asked by some people, "Why does God allow evil?".

God does not 'allow' evil, he allows us to make choices, for the reason just given. We then sometimes deliberately choose evil and spoil God's world or break it into pieces. But evil has not yet managed to triumph completely over good. As more people come to understand the important role which Jesus has in combating evil, goodness will win more and more over evil.

I only said "An apple a day keeps the Doctor away!"

52

That is why it is important that each person can, and must, decide to follow what Jesus tells us is right.

There are people who are very frightened of evil.

Evil ideas do come into our minds sometimes, however much we try to do what is right.

But evil is not stronger than goodness, so we have to ensure that no evil is allowed to get a firm foothold in our own life.

We sometimes need help from other good people, and we should not be afraid to ask for it.

The next words are not in all the services, but are worth thinking about.

In the prayers after Communion, there is usually a reference to God's **grace.**

Grace.

As used in the Bible, 'grace' is a word meaning 'favour' or 'kindness' - which is often undeserved.

Some writers have used the word especially for the kindness which God shows to us when we have done wrong, but this is a more narrow use of the word. We do, however, need to remember that we have no <u>right</u> to receive forgiveness, it is given to us by God's kindness, or 'grace'.

But the word was traditionally used as being an undeserved favour given by someone important to a person who was less important.

(Before eating a meal, right-thinking people may say 'Thank you' to God for God's grace in providing food and other gifts for us. And pray that we use them in the right way. This has become known as 'saying grace'.)

Jesus showed us the 'grace' of God in all He said and did. Even the fact that Jesus came at all was because of God's kindness to us, which we had done nothing to deserve.

I thought you said it needed some GRACE!

53

The final prayer may mention the **'atonement'**.
Atonement.
The meaning is written in the word - **'At one'**.
When we do wrong we cause divisions.
Somehow or other we have to try to get back 'at one' again instead of being divided.
Sometimes we can do this by ourselves, sometimes we need someone to do it for us.
Jesus made us 'at one' with God if we are willing to accept His ways. He also showed us that God is willing to forgive and be 'at one' with us again if we are ready to do so.
(*This we have also seen under* **'Forgive'**.)

There is also sometimes a mention of the **'Passion'** *of Jesus.*
Passion.
In religious language this had nothing to do with kisses, rage or excessive emotion.
It comes from the past form of a Latin word which means 'to suffer'.
So the 'Passion' of Jesus is the cruel time He **suffered** at His crucifixion.

The youth club seemed to have slightly misunderstood 'Passions Sunday'!

*At the end of the service, we usually ask for God's **blessing**.*
Blessing.
This word is translated from the Greek words 'eu' and 'logos', which mean 'beneficial' (or 'prospering') and 'word'. It is sometimes called a 'benediction', which is also associated with the Latin 'bene' and 'dicere' meaning 'well' and 'to speak'.

So by both accounts, a 'blessing' is connected with speaking in a good way which helps something to prosper.

By general use it also came to apply to prosperity which was actually given, as well as just the promise of it.

So when God 'blessed' people it was not merely a question of wishing them well, God might also do something to help them to prosper too.

Through all ages people have asked for God's blessing, and have also blessed each other, (i.e. asked that the person who was blessed might prosper).

It was often done in a solemn way by laying hands on the head of the person to be blessed, all of which made it more personal and more solemn.

And we still ask for God's blessing today.

There is no better way of ending this selection of ideas than to pray that you might be blessed for having studied them.

INDEX